The Wealth Blueprint

How Capitalists Use Debt and
Taxes to Build Financial Freedom

Kendra J.Cowan

Book by the author

- The 7 Money Habits Keeping You Poor
- Unlocking Your Potential
- Embracing Freedom Through Obedience

Copyright

© 2024 **Kendra J. Cowan**. All rights reserved.

This work is copyrighted under the laws of the United States of America and other countries. No part of this work may be reproduced, distributed, or transmitted in any form or by any means, electronic or mechanical, including photocopying, recording, or by any information storage and retrieval system, without written permission from the copyright holder.

Table of contents

Book by the author i

Copyright ii

Table of contents iii

Introduction 1

    The School System's Failure 1

    Why the Rich Pay Less in Taxes 4

Chapter 1: The Foundation of Capitalism 8

    The Boston Tea Party: A Tax Revolt That Shaped America 8

    1913: The Year That Changed Everything 10

    The Connection Between Taxes and Debt 12

Chapter 2: Understanding Taxes and Who Pays the Most 17

    The Four Quadrants of Income 17

    Why the Wealthy Pay Less in Taxes 24

Chapter 3: Capitalism vs. Communism: A Tax Perspective 27

    The Communist Manifesto and Progressive Taxation 28

    Capitalism as Freedom 30

Chapter 4: The Role of Debt in Capitalism 36

    Good Debt vs. Bad Debt: A Tool for Building Wealth 36

    Real-Life Example: Leveraging Debt in Real Estate and Business 38

    Debt as a Tax-Free Wealth Builder 40

Chapter 5: Legal Tax Avoidance for Capitalists 47

    Government Incentives for Capitalists 47

The Tax Code as an Instruction Manual 49

Business and Investment Tax Breaks: Real Estate, Oil, and Beyond 51

Chapter 6: The Capitalist Investor 55

Insider vs. Outsider Investors: The Power of Active Investing 55

Investor Tax Advantages: Why Active Investing Pays More ..57

Case Study: Oil Investments and Their Unique Tax Advantages 59

Chapter 7: Why Small Business Owners Pay the Most in Taxes 64

The Self-Employed Tax Trap: When Freedom Costs You 64

Employee vs. Employer Taxes: The Double Tax Burden 66

Chapter 8: Capitalism in Action: Case Studies 73

Real Estate Investment: The Power of Depreciation 74

Oil and Gas Investments: Drilling for Wealth........................75

Chapter 9: The Global Perspective on Taxes and Entrepreneurship..82

Tax Systems Around the World: The Common Ground.........83

Debunking the Myth: "You Can't Do That Here" 84

Chapter 10: The Future of Capitalism and Tax Strategies..........92

Emerging Tax Strategies: The Role of Technology, Renewable Energy, and Government Priorities 93

How to Stay Ahead: Working with Tax Professionals to Adapt to Changing Laws 96

Conclusion: Embracing Capitalism for Financial Freedom 101

v

Introduction

There's an old American proverb that states, "A fool and his money are soon parted." And it's a sad truth, particularly when you look at what institutions teach—or rather, don't teach—about money. The financial education system in America is flawed. Our children are taught to memorize facts, pass exams, and follow norms, but when it comes to understanding money, debt, or taxes, they are left in the dark. And here's the reality: If you don't understand how money works, money will work against you.

The School System's Failure

Let me ask: Did your education ever teach you how to balance a checkbook? How to invest? Did anyone sit you down and explain the tax code or demonstrate to you the power of leverage? I'm willing to wager that the answer is no. Instead, most of us were told to work diligently, get excellent grades, find a secure job, and save for retirement. That's the advice my sick dad gave me. And it's the advice that most people still adhere to, generation after generation.

But here's the problem: Schools are educating people to become employees. They're not preparing you for financial independence. They're creating laborers, not intellectuals. Employees pay the greatest taxes. They are the backbone of the system, fueling the government's coffers. But why is that? Because institutions don't teach financial education, they teach obedience. They train you to be a cog in the wheel, not the person who owns the wheel.

The truth is, if you want to be wealthy, you must grasp the language of money. It's not taught in education. It's not about algebra, history, or physics. It's about comprehending economic flow, assets, liabilities, taxes, and most importantly, how to make money work for you. This lack of financial education keeps individuals trapped in the rat race. They are working diligently, paying taxes, preserving what little they can, and hoping for a comfortable retirement. But hope is not a plan, and without the proper knowledge, that comfort will never arrive.

The Power of Understanding Money, Debt, and Taxes

Money is an instrument. Just like a hammer or a saw, it can help you construct something amazing if you know how to use it. But without understanding it, money can be as hazardous as a double-edged sword. Debt, for example, is one of the most misconstrued financial instruments. People conceive of debt as something evil, something to be avoided. And while that's true if you're awash in credit card debts, there is also something called positive debt. Good debt places money in your pocket. It's an investment in your future.

The rich know how to use excellent debt to build wealth. They borrow money to acquire assets like real estate, enterprises, or oil wells—things that generate cash flow and appreciate over time. The average individual, meanwhile, borrows to acquire liabilities like vehicles or vacations, which drain their bank accounts.

Debt isn't the enemy but ignorance is the enemy. If you know how to use debt judiciously, it can be a powerful ally in your journey to financial freedom. But if you don't understand it, debt will destroy you, just like it's crushing so many hardworking people today. That's why financial education is so essential. If you don't understand money, debt will operate against you. If you do understand it, debt works for you.

Now, taxes. Let's talk about that, because here's the kicker—taxes are the largest expense in your life. Most people don't realize it, but they're laboring the first three to four months of the year to pay the government. They earn money, pay taxes, and are left with the leftovers. But the wealthy, understand the tax code. And before you assume this is about doing something shady or unlawful, let me be clear—it's not. The wealthy merely know how to operate by the norms that are already written in the tax code.

Why the Rich Pay Less in Taxes

You see, the tax code isn't a consequence; it's a succession of incentives. The government needs people to create employment, develop housing, invest in renewable energy, and keep the economy moving. So, they reward those who do these tasks with tax benefits. The wealthy invest in real estate, establish businesses, and create employment. By doing what the government desires, they get to retain more of their money.

On the other hand, employees—the E quadrant in Robert Kiyosaki's book "Cashflow Quadrant" —pay the highest taxation because they're not taking on the risks that benefit the economy. They work diligently, earn a salary, and pay taxes on that salary. That's it. Their money doesn't multiply. But the wealthy? They invest in items that have tax benefits. Real estate, for example, allows them to depreciate property, which reduces their taxable income. That means they legally keep more money in their wallets.

Here's a basic example: Let's say you invest $1 million in an apartment building. You're providing housing, which the government desires, and in return, you get to write off a portion of the building's value each year through depreciation. That diminishes your taxable income, sometimes down to zero. Meanwhile, the tenants pay rent, which covers the mortgage, and over time, the property appreciates. So, not only are you paying little to no taxes, but your wealth is also expanding.

The average person doesn't even know this is possible because no one teaches them. The wealthy aren't smarter—they're just financially educated. They understand the game of money, and they play it well. And the good news is, you can learn it too.

A Different Way of Thinking

This is where most individuals strike a wall. They think, "I can't do that," or "I don't have that kind of money." But you have to alter your mindset. The affluent think differently. They think in terms of assets, financial flow, and leverage. They ask, "How can I afford this?" not "I can't afford it." They think about how to make money work for them, not how to work harder for money.

So, if you want to cease living paycheck to paycheck, you must start thinking like the wealthy. That begins with understanding the fundamentals of money, debt, and taxes. The instruments are out there, and they are available to anyone willing to learn. You don't have to be a financial savant, but you do have to be willing to think differently.

Once you comprehend how money works, you'll see opportunities everywhere. Instead of feeling confined, you'll feel empowered. And when you start implementing this knowledge, you'll realize that prosperity isn't something reserved for a select few—it's something you can create for yourself.

As the proverb goes, "The best time to plant a tree was twenty years ago." The second greatest time is now." It's never too late to start constructing your financial education. The world needs more people who are financially free, who understand money, and who are using it to construct a better future for themselves and their families.

Remember, it's not about how much money you make. It's about how much you keep, and how hard that money works for you.

Chapter 1: The Foundation of Capitalism

There's an old American proverb that says, "He who knows nothing is closer to the truth than he whose mind is filled with falsehoods." And when it comes to the foundation of capitalism, too many people are operating under falsehoods—especially about money, taxation, and debt. Most of what we've been taught about these subjects is inaccurate or incomplete, and that's by design. The true story is hidden behind years of history and a financial system never intended to serve the average person. To know the truth about capitalism and how to succeed in it, we must first go back to where it all began.

The Boston Tea Party: A Tax Revolt That Shaped America

When we think about the founding of the United States, we often speak about the Declaration of Independence in 1776, but the true beginning of America's journey as a capitalist nation started earlier, in 1773, with the Boston Tea Party. This wasn't just a protest against British tea or even British rule. It was a protest against taxation—specifically, taxation without representation.

At its center, the Boston Tea Party was a tax revolt. The British government imposed costly taxes on products like tea, but the American colonists had no say. They were compelled to pay taxes that funded a government they had no control over. And so, they fought back. They poured 342 chests of British tea into Boston Harbor, sending a message that would reverberate through history: We will not be slaves to taxes.

This event wasn't just a flare for the American Revolution—it was a spark for capitalism. It set the stage for a new kind of society, one where individuals would have the freedom to create their own prosperity, make their own decisions, and retain what they earned. In that instant, the idea of capitalism as we know it today was founded.

Fast forward to modern times, and we're still contending with the same issues. The wealthy realize that taxes are a form of control. They realize that to genuinely be free, you must discover ways to minimize the quantity of money you hand over to the government. The Boston Tea Party taught us that taxation without representation is tyranny. Today, we must understand that unnecessary taxation is just another form of financial servitude.

1913: The Year That Changed Everything

Let's move forward to another defining moment in American financial history: the year 1913. This is a year many people don't know about, but it was a turning point in how money, taxes, and debt operate in this country.

In 1913, two significant events occurred that would eternally shape the financial system: the creation of the Federal Reserve and the passing of the 16th Amendment, which established the federal income tax. These two events are more connected than most people realize. They form the backbone of the system that keeps so many people trapped in the rat race, working diligently but never really moving ahead.

First, let's talk about the Federal Reserve. Most people presume the Federal Reserve is part of the government, but that's not true. It's a private institution. The Federal Reserve is not "federal," it has no reserves, and it's not even really a bank in the traditional sense. What it does, though, is control the money supply. It prints money out of thin air, and that's where the trouble begins.

When the Federal Reserve was created, it profoundly changed how money worked in America. Instead of being secured by gold or silver—something tangible that held value—the dollar became backed by debt. The Federal Reserve could print as much money as it wished, but all of that money was debt. Every dollar that's created is borrowed from the Federal Reserve at interest. That means the U.S. government—and by extension, the American people—are always in debt to the Federal Reserve.

Why does this matter? Because debt is the lifeblood of our financial system. The U.S. dollar itself is debt, and the only way the government can pay back that debt is through taxes. That's why the 16th Amendment, which introduced the federal income tax, was passed in the same year. Taxes became the government's method of paying the interest on the debt it owes to the Federal Reserve. And who pays those taxes? You do.

The Connection Between Taxes and Debt

Here's where most people mistake the point: Debt and taxes are two aspects of the same coin. The U.S. government borrows money from the Federal Reserve, creating debt. To pay that debt back, the government taxes its citizens. But because the money itself is debt, the cycle never ends. The government borrows more, which means it needs to tax more, and round and round we go.

This is why understanding debt is so important. Most people conceive of debt as something to be avoided, something negative. But the truth is, debt is just a tool. It can operate for you or against you, depending on how you use it. The wealthy know how to use debt to their advantage. They borrow money to invest in assets that generate cash flow—things like real estate, businesses, and other income-producing ventures. They use debt to develop wealth.

The typical person, on the other hand, borrows money to purchase liabilities. They take out loans to purchase vehicles, vacations, or even homes that don't generate any income. They end up paying interest on things that don't put money back in their wallets. And then, on top of that, they pay taxes to cover the government's debt.

But the rich? The wealthy understand that taxes are for people who don't understand money. They use the tax code to legally avoid paying more than their reasonable share. They invest in items the government incentivizes—real estate, hydrocarbons, renewable energy, and job creation. And because they are doing what the government desires; they retain more of their money.

Why the Rich Pay Less in Taxes

Most people believe it's unfair that the wealthy pay less in taxes, but the truth is, they're just playing by the rules. The tax code is not designed to penalize the wealthy. It's designed to incentivize investment in the economy. The government needs individuals to establish businesses, create employment, and provide housing. So, it offers tax incentives to those who do these tasks.

If you comprehend how the tax code functions, you can reduce your taxes legally. The rich know this, and they take full advantage. They invest in things that come with tax benefits—things like real estate, which enables them to depreciate the value of their properties and reduce their taxable income. They establish enterprises, which come with a host of deductions. They invest in energy, which comes with its own set of tax benefits.

The average individual, on the other hand, doesn't comprehend the tax code. They earn an income, pay taxes on their wages, and then expend what's left. They don't take advantage of the deductions and credits that are available because they don't know they exist. And so, they end up paying far more in taxes than they need to.

This is why financial education is so essential. If you don't understand how money, debt, and taxes operate, you'll always be at a disadvantage. But if you take the time to learn, you can transform the system to your advantage. You can use debt to build wealth, and you can use the tax code to keep more of what you earn.

A New Way of Thinking About Money

The foundation of capitalism is understanding that money is not just something you earn—it's something you use. The rich don't labor for money. They make money work for them. They use debt to acquire assets that generate income. They use the tax code to legally avoid paying more than they have to. And they keep amassing wealth while paying little to no taxes.

This is the potency of financial education. It grants you the means to see the world differently. It opens your eyes to the possibilities that exist when you comprehend how money, debt, and taxes are interconnected. It allows you to break free from the cycle of working diligently, paying taxes, and never getting ahead.

But it all begins with a transformation in mindset. You have to quit thinking like an employee and start thinking like an entrepreneur. You have to realize that the system is designed to reward those who take risks, invest in assets, and contribute to the economy. It's not about working harder—it's about working wiser.

Remember, entrepreneurship is about freedom. It's about having the freedom to make your own choices, to create your prosperity, and to retain what you earn. But to do that, you need to know the foundation of entrepreneurship. You need to understand how the system functions so that you can use it to your advantage.

In the words of one of my mentors, "Money without financial intelligence is money soon gone." If you want to be genuinely free, you must assume control of your financial education. Learn how money works. Learn how debt works. Learn how taxes operate. And once you do, you'll see that the path to wealth is not as complicated as you've been led to believe.

Chapter 2: Understanding Taxes and Who Pays the Most

As an old Canadian proverb says, "He who seeks the needle must travel through the haystack." And when it comes to taxes, it often feels like you're seeking answers in a vast and confusing world of rules, statistics, and loopholes. But I'm here to tell you that understanding taxes doesn't have to be complicated. Once you know how the system works, you'll see that it's designed to reward certain behaviors—and punish others.

The Four Quadrants of Income

Let's begin by talking about the Four Quadrants of Income. This is the foundation of knowing who pays the most in taxes, and why. In Robert Kiyosaki's book Cashflow Quadrant, he breaks down the four ways individuals earn income: Employees (E), Self-employed (S), Business Owners (B), and Investors (I). Each of these quadrants represents a distinct relationship with money—and, importantly, a different tax bracket. Once you understand which quadrant you fall into, you can see why some people pay a large portion of their income in taxes while others legally avoid them almost entirely.

Employees (E) and the High Cost of Taxes

If you're in the Employee quadrant (E), you have a job. You work for someone else, and you receive a wage in exchange for your time and labor. This is how the majority of individuals receive their income. It's also the quadrant that gets taxed the most.

Think about it: As an employee, your taxes are taken out of your paycheck before you even see the money. That's how the government ensures you pay up first. You're paying income taxes, Social Security taxes, Medicare taxes, and maybe even state and local taxes. In many countries, employees can easily lose 30% to 40% of their income to taxes. You're taxed at the highest rate because you are trading time for money, and the government makes sure it takes its cut before you can even pay your expenses.

Why is this important to understand? Because if you're an employee, you're playing the game at a tremendous disadvantage. You're working diligently, but you're keeping less of what you earn. The tax code is not written to benefit employees—it's written to benefit individuals who take risks, establish businesses, and invest in assets. That's the actuality.

Now, I'm not saying being an employee is bad. We all have to start somewhere. But if your objective is financial freedom, remaining in the Employee quadrant will make that much tougher. The tax system is designed to keep employees laboring for their money, not to help them build fortunes.

The Self-Employed (S): Working Twice as Hard for Less

Next, let's consider the Self-employed quadrant (S). These are the people who say, "I'm tired of working for someone else. I'm going to be my boss!" And while that sounds great in principle, the reality is that many self-employed individuals wind up working harder than they ever did as employees—and they still pay a lot in taxes.

When you're self-employed, you're not just responsible for paying your income taxes—you also have to pay both the employee and employer portions of Social Security and Medicare taxes. That's because, technically, you're both the laborer and the employer. So, instead of paying 6.2% for Social Security and 1.45% for Medicare like employees do, you're paying 12.4% for Social Security and 2.9% for Medicare. That's a significant difference.

And it doesn't stop there. Self-employed individuals also face higher tax rates as their income increases. So, while they might believe they're gaining independence by working for themselves, they're often just working harder, paying more in taxes, and having less time for the things they enjoy.

Many self-employed individuals don't realize this when they start. They think that being their boss will grant them freedom, but they soon find out that they're still trapped—just in a different manner. Instead of being trapped in a cubicle, they're stuck paying high taxes, managing every aspect of their business, and often working more hours than they ever did as employees.

The Business Owner (B): The Tax System Rewards Builders

Now, let's proceed to the Business Owner quadrant (B). This is where things get intriguing. If you own a business with 500 or more employees, you're in the Business Owner quadrant. But here's the critical difference: As a business proprietor, you're not working for money—

your money is working for you. And the tax system rewards that.

You see, the government wants people to create employment. They want businesses to invest in their communities, build infrastructure, and provide employment. So, they offer tax breaks to persons who do these tasks. As a business proprietor, you're able to deduct all types of expenses before you even pay taxes. Salaries, rent, utilities, travel expenses, health benefits—it's all deductible. This means that your taxable income is much lower than what you earn.

For example, let's say you own a business that produces $1 million in revenue. As an employee, you'd be taxed on that full $1 million. But as a business proprietor, you might only be taxed on $100,000 after all your expenses are deducted. That's a significant difference.

And that's not all. The tax system also allows business owners to take advantage of depreciation. If you invest in equipment, buildings, or even certain kinds of vehicles, you can write off a portion of their value every year as they "depreciate." This further reduces your taxable income, allowing you to retain even more of what you earn.

This is why the wealthy pay less in taxes—they know how to use the system to their advantage. They invest in enterprises, they create employment, and they take the risks that the government wants people to take. And in return, they get to retain more of their money.

Investors (I): Making Money Work for You

Finally, we arrive at the Investor quadrant (I). This is where the true magic occurs. Investors don't labor for money—money works for them. And because they are investing in goods that grow in value over time—real estate, stocks, bonds, energy, gold, and other assets—they pay the least in taxes.

Why? Because the government wants individuals to invest in the economy. When you invest in real estate, for example, you're providing accommodation. The government requires that, so they offer tax incentives like depreciation and capital gains tax rebates to encourage people to invest in property.

Similarly, when you invest in businesses or securities, you're providing the capital that allows those businesses to flourish. The government rewards that with reduced tax rates on long-term capital gains, dividends, and other investment income.

Investors also have the advantage of using debt to build wealth. When you borrow money to invest in an asset—like taking out a mortgage to buy real estate—you're using other people's money to develop your wealth. And here's the best part: The interest on that debt is often tax-deductible, meaning you can reduce your taxable income even further. The rich have mastered the art of using debt to develop wealth and decrease taxes. They borrow money to invest in assets that generate cash flow and appreciation, while legally reducing their tax liabilities.

Why the Wealthy Pay Less in Taxes

Now, let's address the query on everyone's mind: Why do the rich pay less in taxes? The answer is simple: They know how the tax system works, and they take advantage of the incentives the government offers.

The tax code is not a consequence of generating money. It's a set of incentives designed to encourage certain behaviors. The government needs individuals to develop businesses, create employment, provide housing, invest in clean energy, and more. So, they reward individuals who do these things with tax benefits.

For example, if you invest in renewable energy—something the government is pressing for right now—you can receive tax credits that reduce your tax liability. If you build affordable housing, you might qualify for special deductions or reimbursements. If you establish a business and hire employees, you can deduct all types of expenses that reduce your taxable income.

In short, the wealthy pay less in taxes because they do what the government wishes them to do. They create employment, invest in the economy, and take risks. And the tax code rewards them for it. The key is that they know the norms of the game, and they execute it well.

The Path to Financial Freedom

So, what does this imply for you? It means that if you want to reduce your tax burden and create wealth, you need to cease thinking like an employee or a self-employed individual. You need to start thinking like a business owner or an investor. You need to realize that the tax system is not your enemy—it's your partner if you know how to use it.

Financial freedom is not about working harder. It's about working intelligently. It's about using the instruments available to you—like the tax code, debt, and investment opportunities—to build wealth and keep more of what you earn. You don't have to be wealthy to start—anyone can transition from the E or S quadrant to the B or I quadrant with the proper knowledge and mindset.

Chapter 3: Capitalism vs. Communism: A Tax Perspective

There's an old African proverb that says, "The child who is not embraced by the village will burn it down to feel its warmth." It talks to a fundamental human need to be seen, heard, and valued. This same principle pertains to how societies structure themselves, particularly when it comes to taxes and wealth. When people feel oppressed or neglected by a system that works against them, they seek out alternatives—even if those alternatives bring greater harm than good.

This is where the ideological confrontation between capitalism and communism comes in, and nowhere is that conflict more evident than in the way these two systems approach taxes. Today, we're going to talk about the tax perspective from these two drastically different philosophies—one that leads to freedom, and the other that leads to control.

The Communist Manifesto and Progressive Taxation

Let's begin by taking a look at The Communist Manifesto, written by Karl Marx in 1848. Marx's ideas shaped the foundation of communism, and they were constructed on the belief that the wealthy exploited the poor. His solution? Erase the differences between the classes by redistributing wealth from the wealthy to the impoverished. To do this, he proposed many strategies, but one of the most important was the implementation of a progressive income tax.

Now, what is a progressive income tax? It's a tax system where the more money you earn, the higher the percentage of your income you pay in taxes. Sounds familiar, right? That's because it's the same system used in most countries today, including the United States.

The concept behind progressive taxation is that the wealthy should contribute more to society because they have more. On the surface, it sounds fair—those who have more should give more. But when you probe deeper, you realize that progressive taxation is not about equity. It's about control.

Marx's vision was not just to tax the wealthy more; it was to use those taxes to take away the power of the wealthiest and redistribute it to the government. That's the core of communism—centralized control. In this system, the government decides how much everyone should have, and it employs taxes to make sure wealth is evenly distributed.

But here's the problem: In a system where wealth is forcibly removed from one group and transferred to another, you're not empowering people—you're enslaving them. When the government takes more and more through taxes, it removes away the incentive for people to work harder, establish businesses, or invest. Why should someone take risks or innovate when the fruits of their labor will just be taken away?

Progressive taxation, as proposed in The Communist Manifesto, isn't about lifting individuals. It's about pulling individuals down to a level where they are simpler to control. And that's the fundamental difference between communism and capitalism.

Capitalism as Freedom

Now, let's talk about capitalism, which I sincerely believe is the path to financial freedom. At its essence, capitalism is about choice. It's about the freedom to determine what you do with your money, your time, and your talents. It's about taking risks and reaping the rewards—or learning from the setbacks. Capitalism empowers individuals to create their destinies, and a huge part of that is understanding how to reduce your tax burden legally, allowing you to retain more of what you earn.

In capitalism, taxes still exist, but the system is designed to recompense those who take risks, create employment, and invest in the economy. The government grants tax breaks and incentives to business owners, investors, and those who contribute to the development of the economy because, essentially, the government needs those people to keep the engine running. Without them, there are no jobs, no innovation, no progress.

Let's be clear: In a capitalist system, the tax code is not a sanction. It's a set of instructions—a guide to help you comprehend how to keep more of your money legally. The tax code rewards those who create value for others, whether that's by establishing enterprises, investing in real estate, or funding new technology. The more you contribute to the economy, the more you are allowed to retain.

That's the difference between capitalism and communism. In communism, the government decides how much you get to retain. In capitalism, you determine how much you get to keep by how much value you create. It's a system that encourages growth and rewards effort, while communism stifles it.

Progressive Taxation vs. Flat Tax

Now, you might be pondering, "If capitalism is about freedom, why do we still have progressive taxation in capitalist countries?" That's a great question, and the answer goes back to a misunderstanding about justice.

In a capitalist society, people often contend that progressive taxes are necessary to balance out the inequality that comes with wealth accumulation. They believe that without these taxes, the wealthy will get wealthier while the impoverished get poorer. But this thinking comes from the same location Marx's ideas emerged from—a scarcity mindset. It's the belief that wealth is a zero-sum game, that for one individual to become wealthy, someone else must become poor.

But prosperity is not a pie with only so many portions to go around. Wealth can be created. In fact, that's what capitalism does—it creates wealth by encouraging innovation, risk-taking, and entrepreneurship. Progressive taxation doesn't equalize the playing field—it penalizes the very individuals who are creating value and wealth for everyone else.

A preferable alternative to progressive taxation would be a flat tax—a system where everyone pays the same percentage of their income, no matter how much they make. This system is equitable because everyone contributes the same proportion of their earnings, and it doesn't punish accomplishment. A flat tax encourages people to work harder, establish enterprises, and invest, knowing that they won't be penalized for their efforts with higher taxes. It's a system that corresponds with the principles of capitalism—freedom, fairness, and opportunity.

Why Taxes Matter

The reason I'm talking about taxes so much is that they're the largest expense in most people's lives. If you're not paying attention to how taxes affect your income, you're going to be working harder and retaining less of what you earn. And here's the thing: The wealthy understand this. They know that taxes are a tool to be used, not a burden to be endured.

The wealthy don't avoid taxes because they're dishonest or greedy—they avoid taxes because they understand the tax code. They realize that the government provides tax incentives to those who invest in things that benefit society—real estate, renewable energy, and job creation. They know that by using these incentives, they can legally reduce their tax burden and keep more of their money.

This is why the affluent pay less in taxation. It's not because they're abusing the system. It's because they're playing the game the correct way. They know the norms, and they use them to their advantage. And here's the excellent news: You can do the same thing.

The Freedom to Choose

At the end of the day, capitalism is about choice. It's about having the freedom to choose how you live your life, how you earn your money, and how you spend it. In a capitalist system, you have the power to make decisions that impact your financial future. You can choose to invest in assets that rise in value. You can choose to establish businesses that create employment. And you can choose to use the tax code to keep more of what you earn.

Communism, on the other hand, is about removing that choice away. It's about centralizing control in the hands of the government, with the notion that everyone should have the same, regardless of how hard they work or how much value they create. But here's the truth: When the government takes away your ability to create and keep wealth, it takes away your freedom.

As my wealthy dad once told me, "The more the government controls your money, the less freedom you have." And that's why I'm such a strong believer in capitalism. It's not ideal, but it's the system that gives you the most freedom to construct your destiny. And when you comprehend how the tax system works, you'll see that capitalism isn't about taking from the impoverished and giving to the wealthy. It's about creating value, developing wealth, and rewarding those who take risks.

Chapter 4: The Role of Debt in Capitalism

"Debt is an instrument. The only question is, who is using it?" This is something I've said for years, and it's a truth most people need to hear over and over. When most people think of debt, they think of stress, restless nights, and anxiety. They see debt as a weight dragging them down, keeping them trapped in a financial trap. But what if I told you that debt isn't the problem? It's how you use it that makes the difference. There's good debt and bad debt. The wealthy understand this difference and use debt as a tool to develop their fortunes. The typical person, unfortunately, doesn't. And that's what keeps them working harder for less.

Good Debt vs. Bad Debt: A Tool for Building Wealth

Let's commence with the basics: Good debt versus poor debt. This is a concept that most people have never been taught. In school, we're told that debt is something to avoid at all costs. The common wisdom is, "Pay off your debts and live debt-free." But the fact is, debt can be a potent tool when used correctly.

Bad debt is the kind of debt that drains money out of your purse. It's debt that doesn't generate any income and only consumes your resources. Think of credit card debt, auto loans, or financing a vacation. When you take on bad debt, you're borrowing money to pay for things that don't place money back in your purse. You're spending tomorrow's income on today's expenses, and all you're left with is a bill to pay, plus interest.

But **good debt** is an altogether different issue. Good debt is debt that places money in your purse. It's debt that you use to acquire assets that generate income or increase in value over time. Wealthy people realize that they don't need to use their own money to develop wealth. They use other people's money—through acceptable debt—to invest in real estate, businesses, and other cash-flowing assets.

Here's the key: Good debt makes you wealthier. Bad debt makes you impoverished. If you can comprehend this one concept, you'll start to see how the wealthy use debt to get ahead, while the poor and middle class remain stuck. It's not about avoiding debt; it's about learning how to use it prudently.

Real-Life Example: Leveraging Debt in Real Estate and Business

Let me give you a real-life example of how I've used excellent debt to build prosperity in real estate. When I invest in real estate, I rarely, if ever, pay for the entire property in cash. Instead, I leverage debt to acquire income-producing properties.

suppose you want to purchase a $1 million apartment building. Now, most people would say, "I need $1 million to buy this property." But that's not how the wealthy think. Instead, I think, "How can I use as little of my own money as possible to acquire this asset?"

So, let's suppose I take out a loan for $800,000 to acquire the property, and I invest $200,000 of my own money. Now, I own a $1 million asset, but I've only used $200,000 of my own money. The occupants who reside in the apartment building pay rent, which covers the mortgage, and operating expenses, and even generates cash flow. The property also appreciates over time.

What's happening here? The tenants are paying off the debt, not me. I'm using debt to acquire an asset that places money in my pocket every month. And over time, as the property value increases, my equity in the property rises. I've essentially used other people's money (the banks and the tenants') to establish prosperity for myself. That's the potency of positive debt.

This same principle pertains to commerce. Many successful entrepreneurs use debt to finance the growth of their enterprises. Instead of using all their own money to get started, they take out loans or raise capital, allowing them to grow quicker than they could with just their resources. They use the profits from the business to pay off the debt while building a company that generates more revenue over time.

Debt as a Tax-Free Wealth Builder

Now, here's where things get interesting: Debt is one of the most potent, tax-free wealth producers out there. Let me explain how.

When you earn income from a job, you're taxed on it. The more you make, the more you pay in taxes. But when you borrow money—whether it's to acquire real estate or develop a business—that borrowed money is not taxable. You don't pay taxes on debt. That's because debt isn't deemed income—it's considered a liability.

Let's return to the example of the apartment building. I borrowed $800,000 to purchase the property, and I'm not paying taxes on that $800,000 because it's a loan, not income. Over time, the property appreciates. Let's suppose, that after a few years, the building is now worth $1.5 million, and I decided to refinance it. I take out a new loan for $1.2 million. I pay off the original $800,000 loan, and I'm left with $400,000 in cash. That $400,000 is mine to retain, and here's the greatest part: It's tax-free.

Why? Because the $400,000 isn't considered income—it's considered debt. I haven't sold the property, so I haven't realized any capital gains. I've merely borrowed against the increased value of the property, and the government doesn't tax debt.

This is one of the most powerful strategies the wealthy use to create wealth without paying taxes. They borrow against their assets—whether it's real estate, securities, or businesses—and use that debt to finance their lifestyle or reinvest in more assets. Meanwhile, they're not paying income taxes on that borrowed money.

Compare that to someone in the Employee quadrant, who works diligently for a paycheck and sees a significant portion of their income taken away in taxes before they even see it. The difference is clear: The affluent use debt to build wealth and avoid taxes, while the impoverished and middle class work harder, pay more taxes, and struggle to get ahead.

Changing Your Mindset About Debt

Now, I know some of you might be thinking, "This sounds risky." And you're right—using debt does come with dangers. But every investment comes with hazards.

The difference is that the rich comprehend how to manage risk and use it to their advantage. They don't dread debt—they respect it. They know how to use excellent debt to acquire assets that generate income and increase in value over time.

The average individual, on the other hand, has been taught to dread debt. They've been told that all debt is evil and that the path to financial security is to live debt-free. But as I've said many times, living debt-free doesn't mean you're financially free. It just means you're playing it safe. And playing it carefully won't get you to financial liberation.

The key is to alter your perspective about debt. Don't think of it as something to avoid—think of it as a tool to be used judiciously. Understand the difference between good debt and bad debt, and focus on using good debt to acquire assets that place money in your purse. The more assets you acquire, the more affluent you become. And the greatest part is, you're using other people's money to do it.

Learning to Leverage Debt

Leverage is the key to developing prosperity. Leverage allows you to control more assets with less of your own money. When you use leverage, you multiply your

power to develop wealth, because you're using borrowed money to generate income and grow your assets. Think of it this way: If you only invest with your own money, you're limited by how much cash you have on hand. But when you use debt as leverage, you can control larger assets, develop more wealth, and do it quickly.

Let's return to the apartment building example. By investing $200,000 of your own money into a $1 million property, you're leveraging your investment. Instead of being bound with only what you can buy outright, you're using debt to gain control over a much larger asset. The benefit of leverage is that it allows you to control 100% of the property, even though you've only invested 20% of the money. And as the property appreciates, you benefit from 100% of that appreciation, not just the portion you paid for.

This is how the wealthy conceive. They're not frightened of debt; they embrace it because they comprehend how to use it to their advantage. They use debt to buy assets, and those assets generate income, appreciate over time, and provide tax benefits. They let debt work for them, not against them.

Debt and Risk Management

Of course, you can't talk about debt without addressing risk. Debt does come with risk, and that's why it's necessary to use it prudently. The key is not to over-leverage yourself. Too much debt can be hazardous if your investments don't generate enough income to cover your payments. But when managed correctly, debt is a tool that can help you develop tremendous wealth.

The wealthy know how to manage risk. They don't overextend themselves. They make sure that the income from their investments—whether it's rental income from real estate or profits from a business—covers their debt payments and still leaves them with positive cash flow. They have safety measures in place, such as reserves or contingency plans, to ensure they can withstand any storms that come their way.

The average individual, on the other hand, often doesn't know the concept of calculated risk. They've been taught to avoid risk wholly, and in doing so, they avoid opportunities as well. But here's the truth: There's risk in everything you do. There's a risk in having a job—your employer could go out of business, you could get fired off, or the economy could take a downturn. There's a risk in retaining your money in a savings account—inflation could take away the value of your money. So, the true question isn't whether there's risk, but how you manage it.

The wealthy know how to manage risk and use it to their advantage. They know how to leverage debt, diversify their investments, and create multiple streams of income so they're not reliant on any one source. They take calculated risks, and that's why they continue to grow their wealth while others remain trapped.

Debt as Freedom

One of the greatest misunderstandings about debt is that it confines you. Most people think of debt as something that limits their freedom, but when used correctly, debt can give you more freedom. How? By enabling you to acquire assets that generate passive income.

Passive income is money that comes in without you having to labor for it. It's the rent payments from your tenants, the dividends from your investments, or the profits from your business. When you have enough passive income to cover your living expenses, you've achieved financial liberation. Debt is often the instrument that helps you get there.

Think about it: If you use debt to purchase a rental property that generates positive cash flow every month, that's money you're earning without having to work for it. As you acquire more properties or investments.

Chapter 5: Legal Tax Avoidance for Capitalists

"The more you give the government what it wants, the more you get to keep what you earn." This is one of the biggest secrets the wealthy understand about taxes, but it's something most people never learn. They're too occupied thinking that taxes are some unavoidable burdens. But the reality is, the tax code isn't intended to punish you—it's meant to guide you. Once you comprehend this, you'll see that the government genuinely wants you to avoid taxes. Yes, you heard that correctly. If you play by the rules and do what the government needs, you'll legally reduce your taxes, often to nil.

Government Incentives for Capitalists

Here's the first thing you need to understand: The government is not your enemy. In fact, it's your companion. The tax code is written in a way that rewards individuals who do things that help the country develop and thrive. Things like creating employment, investing in renewable energy, building affordable housing, and developing novel technologies.

Let me explain why. The government has a vast to-do list, but they don't have the time, expertise, or resources to do everything themselves. So, they rely on private individuals and businesses—capitalists—to get the task done. And they offer tax breaks and incentives to those who stand up and aid. This is why the wealthy pay less in taxation. It's not because they're manipulating the system; it's because they're doing what the system desires.

For example, if you create jobs by establishing a business, you're reducing the government's unemployment problem. So, the tax code rewards you with deductions and credits for employing laborers, providing them with health advantages and even training them. The government needs people to work, and they're glad to grant you taxation relief if you help them out.

If you invest in renewable energy, like solar or wind power, you're helping the government meet its sustainable energy objectives. So, they offer tax credits to individuals who install solar panels or invest in energy-efficient buildings. You're assisting the government achieve its objectives, and they reward you by reducing your taxes.

This is how capitalism functions in harmony with government objectives. You assist the government achieve what it can't do on its own, and in return, you retain more of your money. It's a win-win.

The Tax Code as an Instruction Manual

Most people see the tax code as this complex, perplexing document loaded with traps and penalties. But that's not how the rich see it. They see it as an instruction manual. The tax code is replete with incentives that tell you exactly what the government wants you to do. And if you obey those instructions, you pay less in taxes. It's that straightforward.

Let's be clear: The tax code is not out to get you. It's designed to steer behavior. It's the government's way of saying, "If you do this, we'll let you keep more of your money. If you don't, you'll pay more in taxes." Once you grasp that, the whole system begins to make sense.

Here's an excellent analogy: Imagine you're playing a board game, but you never bothered to read the rulebook. You just keep moving your pieces around the board, hoping you'll somehow prevail. That's how most people approach taxes—they don't know the regulations, so they end up paying more than they should. But the wealthy? They've read the rulebook. They know how to play the game, and they use the laws to their advantage.

For example, did you know that if you invest in real estate, you can write off the depreciation of your property every year? Even though your property might truly be increasing in value, the tax code allows you to regard it as if it's losing value, which reduces your taxable income. The government encourages people to invest in housing because it helps address their housing crisis. So, they give you a reprieve for doing it.

Or let's suppose you own a business. The tax code allows you to deduct ordinary and necessary business expenses—things like rent, equipment, salaries, and travel. Why? Because you're assisting the economy by running a business, creating employment, and contributing to the country's GDP. The government doesn't want to tax you significantly for doing something they need, so they give you deductions that lower your taxable income.

Business and Investment Tax Breaks: Real Estate, Oil, and Beyond

The tax code is crammed with incentives for individuals who invest in certain areas. Real estate, hydrocarbons, and renewable energy are just a few examples. Let's look at how these operate.

Real Estate: When you invest in real estate, you're not just purchasing property—you're creating housing, something the government needs more of. So, they reward you with some extraordinary tax benefits. One of the largest is depreciation. Even though your property is likely increasing in value, the tax code allows you to depreciate it—essentially, you're writing off the building's wear and tear over time. This diminishes your taxable income, even though the property might be worth more than when you purchased it. And here's another benefit: If you decide to sell the property later, you can use a tax strategy called a 1031 exchange, which allows you to delay paying capital Gains taxes if you reinvest the earnings in another property. This enables you to keep expanding your portfolio without getting hit with taxes.

Oil and Gas: The government also requires energy, and they offer enormous tax breaks to those who invest in oil and gas. If you invest in oil extraction, you can write off a substantial portion of your investment through something called intangible drilling costs. These are expenses like labor and apparatus that are necessary to explore for oil. You can write off up to 100% of these expenditures in the first year, significantly reducing your taxable income. And here's the kicker: The income you generate from oil wells is often taxed at a lower rate than conventional income. Why? Because the government requires oil and gas production to keep the country operating. They don't want to punish you for helping them out.

Renewable Energy: As the world moves towards healthier energy, the government is pressing hard for investments in solar, wind, and other renewable sources. To encourage individuals to invest in these technologies, they offer tax credits and deductions. If you install solar panels on your property, you could qualify for the Investment Tax Credit (ITC), which allows you to deduct 26% of the cost of installation from your federal taxes. Not only are you reducing your tax bill, but you're also saving money on energy costs, and possibly even earning money if your system generates more power than you need.

The Wealthy Don't Cheat—They Play by the Rules

One of the biggest misconceptions about the wealthy is that they don't pay their due share of taxes. But the truth is, they're just playing by the rules. They've read the tax code—they've studied the rulebook—and they're using it to their advantage. The government is the one setting the norms, and the wealthy are merely following them.

It's essential to realize that these tax breaks and incentives are available to anyone who chooses to take advantage of them. You don't have to be a billionaire to benefit from the tax code. You just have to comprehend how it works and be willing to play by the rules.

So, if you want to reduce your tax burden legally, start thinking like a capitalist. Ask yourself, "What does the government need, and how can I help provide it?" The government will reward you for stepping up and assisting in the solution of their issues, whether it is through job creation, real estate investment, or supporting renewable energy programs. And in return, you'll keep more of your money.

Chapter 6: The Capitalist Investor

"The fool looks for gain, but the wise build wealth." This aphorism holds in every corner of life, but particularly in investing. The difference between merely gaining money and building lasting wealth is one of the key lessons of capitalism, and it's a lesson every investor must learn if they want to succeed. Investing, like anything, has guidelines. And one of the most essential principles is knowing the difference between being an insider investor and an outsider. Once you grasp that difference, you can start using the system to build actual wealth while also taking advantage of the tax breaks the government has built into the system.

Insider vs. Outsider Investors: The Power of Active Investing

Most individuals assume investing is all about the stock market. They've been taught that to expand their wealth, they need to put their money into equities, bonds, or mutual funds and watch it grow over time. This is what I term passive investing. You place your money in someone else's hands—whether it's a company, a fund manager, or the stock market itself—and you pray for the best.

That's what the preponderance of people does. They buy equities, bonds, or mutual funds through their 401(k)s or IRAs, believing that's the key to wealth. But here's the truth: The stock market doesn't make you rich. It makes the insiders wealthy. When you're purchasing equities or bonds, you're an outsider. You don't control the company, you don't make decisions, and you're at the mercy of whatever occurs in the market. You may see gains, but you're not genuinely in control. You're just a passenger on someone else's journey.

On the other hand, insider investors—those who are actively engaged in their investments—build genuine wealth because they're in the driver's seat. An insider investor understands how to control their money, where to place it, and how to make it grow. These investors are involved in real estate, oil, gas, and enterprises where they have more influence over their outcomes. They're not waiting for stock prices to rise or fall—they're making moves to increase their fortunes.

When you invest in real estate, for example, you have control. You determine which properties to purchase, how to enhance them, and how to increase their cash flow. You leverage debt to acquire assets, and you build equity over time. The same goes for energy investments. As an insider, you're part of the decision-making process, and you benefit from tax incentives that passive investors can only dream of.

Investor Tax Advantages: Why Active Investing Pays More

One of the greatest advantages of being an insider investor is the tax benefits. The tax code is structured in a way that rewards individuals who actively invest in goods that benefit the economy—like real estate, oil, and businesses. These sectors create employment, provide housing, and generate energy, all things the government requires. And because the government desires more of that, they offer tax benefits to those who help make it happen.

Let's begin with real estate. As an active real estate investor, you can take advantage of depreciation. Depreciation allows you to write off the value of your property over time, even though it may be appreciating. This is an enormous tax advantage that can reduce your taxable income significantly. If you're investing in rental properties, you can also deduct expenses like mortgage interest, property management fees, maintenance, and even travel related to your property. That's a lot of money you get to keep because the tax code rewards you for providing housing.

Now let's talk about oil and gas investments. This is one of the most tax-advantaged sectors for investors. When you invest in oil drilling, you can write off a significant portion of your investment through something called intangible drilling costs. These are expenses related to labor, apparatus, and other necessary costs of excavating for oil. You can write off up to 100%

of these expenditures in the first year. That means you're investing in a high-return sector while substantially reducing your taxable income. On top of that, the income you earn from oil production is often taxed at a lower rate than regular income because of something called depletion allowances.

By actively investing in oil or real estate, you're not just expanding your wealth through the appreciation of the asset—you're also reducing the taxes you pay. That's how the wealthy keep more of their money. They use the tax code to their advantage, and they invest in areas where they can both expand their wealth and legally avoid taxes.

Case Study: Oil Investments and Their Unique Tax Advantages

Let me give you a real-world example of how investing in oil can be a game-changer for building wealth and reducing taxes. A few years ago, I partnered with a group of investors to explore oil in Texas. It wasn't my first time investing in oil, but each time I'm reminded of just how potent this sector is for growing wealth.

The investment required $1 million upfront, and we used **intangible drilling costs** to write off 85% of that investment in the first year. That means we were able to reduce our taxable income by $850,000 in that first year alone. Now, compare that to someone who makes $1 million in remuneration at their employment. They'd be paying upwards of 40% in taxes on that income, which is $400,000 straight off the top. As oil investors, we not only reduced our tax bill substantially, but we also began earning income from the oil wells almost immediately.

Here's the greatest part: The income we earn from oil isn't taxed the same way as conventional income. Thanks to **depletion allowances**, a portion of the oil we extract is considered to be "used up" over time, which means we're able to write off a percentage of the income we earn from selling it. So, while someone else might be paying 40% in taxes on their compensation, we're paying far less on our hydrocarbon income.

But it doesn't stop there. As the wells continue to produce oil, the cash flow continues flowing in, year after year. And since we've already written off the preponderance of the investment, most of that income is unadulterated profit—tax-advantaged profit. This is the leverage of being an insider investor in a sector like energy. You get to leverage the government's need for energy, take advantage of the tax code, and build long-term wealth.

Changing Your Mindset About Investing

I know some of you might be thinking, "This sounds great, but I don't have $1 million to invest in oil." And that's all right. You don't need to start with millions to begin thinking like an insider investor. The key is to alter your perspective from being a passive investor—someone who just throws money into stocks or mutual funds and wishes for the best—to be an active investor, someone who takes control of their financial future.

You can start modestly. Maybe it's a rental property that generates monthly cash flow and provides you tax benefits through depreciation. Maybe it's investing in a local business that you believe in and can help thrive. Or maybe it's collaborating with other investors to get involved in larger ventures like oil or commercial real estate. The point is, that being a confidential investor grants you control. And when you're in control, you're not just praying for gains—you're accumulating wealth intentionally.

The wealthy don't get prosperous by sitting on the periphery. They get wealthy by getting involved, by taking calculated risks, and by using the tax code to their advantage. And here's the thing: The tax code is written for everyone. It's not just for the rich. It's for anyone willing to understand how it works and use it to their advantage.

The Path Forward

As a capitalist investor, your task is to grasp the rules of the game and use them to build wealth. That means knowing the difference between being an insider and an interloper. It means understanding the tax advantages that come with being an active investor. And it means taking control of your financial future by investing in areas that offer long-term growth and tax savings.

Remember, the government wants you to invest in goods that benefit the economy—housing, electricity, businesses. And they're willing to reward you for doing so. The tax code is replete with opportunities for those who are willing to play the game. The question is, are you ready to stand up and start investing like a capitalist?

As the adage says, "He who cuts wood will be warmed twice." The same is true in investing. When you invest prudently, you not only grow your wealth but also reap the rewards of tax advantages that let you retain more of what you earn. Don't linger on the sidelines. Become an insider, take control, and start building wealth today.

Chapter 7: Why Small Business Owners Pay the Most in Taxes

"The path is long, but the reward is greater at the end." This old saying resonates profoundly when we talk about small business proprietors and taxes. Many people believe that establishing their own business is the key to financial liberation. They think, "If I work for myself, I'll get to keep more of my money, and I won't have to answer to anyone else." That's the ideal, right? But the actuality is often far different. The truth is, many small businesses proprietors wind up paying more in taxes than they did when they were employees. It's a challenging lesson to learn, but one that must be understood if you're sincere about establishing genuine wealth.

The Self-Employed Tax Trap: When Freedom Costs You

Starting your own business sounds like a ticket to liberation. You get to set your own hours, be your boss, and, in principle, retain all the money you earn. But then tax season rolls around, and abruptly, that freedom begins feeling like a burden. Many small business owners get a harsh awakening when they realize that being self-employed means paying more in taxes, not less.

Here's what most individuals don't understand: When you're self-employed, you don't just pay income tax—you also pay self-employment tax. This is the tax that covers Social Security and Medicare, which, as an employee, is usually divided between you and your employer. But when you're self-employed, you are both the employee and the employer. That means you're responsible for both aspects of that tax—12.4% for Social Security and 2.9% for Medicare. That's a total of 15.3% of your income going directly to the government before you even factor in federal and state income taxes.

While being self-employed might feel like a step toward financial independence, it can feel like taking on a larger tax burden. Instead of retaining more of what you earn, you're handing over a larger percentage to Uncle Sam. That's the self-employed tax pitfall, and it's one of the reasons why many small business proprietors struggle to get ahead.

But that's not all. When you're self-employed, you're also responsible for conducting your own health insurance, retirement savings, and other benefits that would typically be provided by an employer. These additional costs cut into your profits and make it even tougher to build wealth.

Employee vs. Employer Taxes: The Double Tax Burden

Let's break it down even further. When you're an employee, your employer covers half of your Social Security and Medicare taxes, as well as other expenses like unemployment insurance and workers' compensation. You might not see it on your paycheck, but your employer is paying a significant portion of these taxes on your behalf. As a result, your overall tax burden is lower because you're only responsible for half of the payroll taxes.

But when you become self-employed, that responsibility falls squarely on your shoulders. You are now the employer, which means you pay both the employer and employee portions of these taxes. That's where the double tax burden enters into action.

For example, let's assume you're an employee earning $100,000 a year. You're responsible for paying 6.2% of your income toward Social Security and 1.45% for Medicare. That's a total of 7.65% or $7,650 in taxes. Your employer is responsible for matching that, paying another $7,650 on your behalf.

But if you're self-employed and earning $100,000, you're responsible for both aspects. You'll pay the full 12.4% for Social Security and 2.9% for Medicare. That's a total of $15,300—double what you would pay as an employee. And that's before you even think about income taxes.

This is the harsh reality many small businesses owners face. They thought starting their own business would mean paying less in taxes, but in fact, they end up paying more because they're responsible for both sides of the tax equation. This is one of the biggest reasons why so many small businesses struggle to grow. They're being hit with taxes from both directions, and it's taking a serious toll on their bottom line.

The Cost of Freedom: Is It Worth It?

Now, you might be thinking, "Why would anyone want to start their own business if the tax burden is so high?" And that's a valid question. But here's the thing: Despite the higher taxes, being a small business owner can still lead to financial freedom—if you know how to play the game.

The key is understanding how to minimize your tax burden and maximize your profits. Just because you're paying more in taxes doesn't mean you can't find ways to reduce those taxes legally. That's where savvy tax planning comes in.

As a business owner, you have access to tax deductions that employees don't. You can write off expenses related to your business, like office rent, supplies, travel, and even a portion of your home if you operate from home. You can also deduct health insurance premiums, retirement contributions, and certain startup expenditures. These deductions can substantially reduce your taxable income, allowing you to retain more of what you earn.

But here's the catch: Many small business owners don't take full advantage of these deductions because they don't know how. They don't have the proper financial education, and they're too occupied running their business to focus on tax strategy. As a result, they end up paying more in taxes than they should.

Why Self-Employed Professionals Get Hit the Hardest

This double tax burden is particularly tough on self-employed professionals—people like physicians, lawyers, accountants, and consultants. These individuals often earn high incomes, but they also confront high tax expenses because they're responsible for both sides of the tax equation. And because they're typically providing services rather than selling products, their administrative costs are lower, which means they have fewer deductions to offset their income.

For example, let's suppose you're a self-employed attorney earning $200,000 a year. You're responsible for paying both the employer and employee portions of Social Security and Medicare, which comes to $30,600. That's a large chunk of your income going directly to taxes before you even pay your federal and state income taxes.

In addition to that, you're responsible for covering your own health insurance, retirement savings, and other benefits that employees typically receive from their employers. And because you're operating a service-based business, you might not have as many expenses to deduct, which means your taxable income remains high.

This is why so many self-employed professionals wind up feeling constrained. They're working diligently, earning a decent income, but they're paying so much in taxes that they can't seem to get ahead. It's frustrating, and its why financial education is so essential for anyone who's thinking about launching their own business.

The Solution: Think Like a Capitalist

So, what's the solution? How do you avoid the self-employed tax pitfall and start retaining more of what you earn? The answer is simple: You need to start thinking like a capitalist.

Capitalists don't labor for money—they make money work for them. They don't get caught in the mentality of trading time for dollars. Instead, they focus on establishing assets that generate passive income and offer tax advantages. And they use the tax code to their advantage, reducing their tax burden while accumulating long-term wealth.

For small business proprietors, this means thinking beyond just providing a service or selling a product. It means creating a business that can operate without you, one that generates income even when you're not actively working. It means investing in real estate, energy, or other ventures that offer tax benefits and long-term growth potential.

It also means taking advantage of every deduction and tax incentive available to you. Hire a competent accountant or tax advisor who understands the tax code and can help you minimize your tax burden. Don't be reluctant to invest in your financial education, because the more you know about taxes, the more money you'll retain.

Freedom Isn't Free

The path to financial freedom is not simple, but it's worth it. Being a small business owner comes with challenges—especially when it comes to taxes—but those challenges can be overcome with the right mindset and the right strategies.

The key is to cease thinking like an employee and start thinking like a capitalist. Learn how to use the tax code to your advantage, build assets that generate income, and take control of your financial future.

As the proverb says, "Great oaks from little acorns grow." It may require time and effort, but the rewards are worth it in the end.

Chapter 8: Capitalism in Action: Case Studies

"The best time to plant a tree was 20 years ago. The second-best time is now." These proverb holds, particularly when it comes to investing and taking advantage of opportunities. The beauty of entrepreneurship is that it offers anyone the opportunity to build wealth, provided they know how the system functions and how to leverage it to their advantage. Today, I want to take you through real-world examples of entrepreneurship in action. We'll still look at how real estate, oil and gas, and large enterprises use the tax code as a tool for building wealth. These case studies will show you that the tax system is not a trap—it's a guidebook, compensating those who contribute to the economy in meaningful ways.

Real Estate Investment: The Power of Depreciation

Let me begin with one of the greatest tools for building wealth in entrepreneurship: **real estate**. I've always been a strong advocate for investing in real estate because it's one of the few assets where you can leverage debt to develop wealth, create cash flow, and use the tax code to your advantage. One of the greatest tax benefits in real estate comes in the form of depreciation.

Depreciation enables real estate investors to reduce their taxable income by deducting the "wear and tear" on a property over time. Here's the brilliance of it: even though the property is presumably appreciating, the government allows you to write off a portion of that value each year as if it's losing value. This creates a potent tool for reducing taxes, even while your wealth is expanding.

Let me give you a basic example. Say you purchase a $1 million apartment building. The IRS enables you to depreciate the building over 27.5 years. That means you can deduct roughly $36,364 every year as depreciation. So, if you're earning $50,000 in rental income from that property, you can subtract that $36,364 from your taxable income, leaving you with only $13,636 in taxable income. This dramatically reduces your tax liability.

And that's just one property. Now imagine you own multiple properties, all generating income, and all benefiting from depreciation. You can see how potent this tax benefit becomes. Depreciation can even offset other forms of income, reducing your overall tax burden.

Real estate is also a fantastic hedge against inflation because, as the cost-of-living increases, so do rents, which enhances your cash flow. In the long term, your tenants are paying off your mortgage while your property appreciates, and you're paying little to no taxes on that cash flow due to depreciation. That's how real estate makes fortunes, and the tax benefits are a significant part of that equation.

Oil and Gas Investments: Drilling for Wealth

Now, let's transfer focus to another sector where savvy investors use the tax code to build wealth: oil and gas. Most people think of oil as a volatile commodity, but those who understand how to invest in oil know that it can be a gold mine—not just because of the potential for high returns, but because of the tax benefits.

There are two primary methods to invest in oil: you can either invest in oil companies by purchasing stocks, or you can invest directly in drilling operations. And let me tell you, drilling for oil has far greater tax advantages than merely purchasing stock in ExxonMobil or Chevron.

When you invest in an oil drilling operation, you get to take advantage of something called intangible drilling costs (IDCs). These are costs associated with the labor, materials, and apparatus required to construct the well. What's extraordinary is that you can write off up to 100% of these expenditures in the first year. This means that if you invest $100,000 in a drilling operation, you can deduct that entire amount from your taxable income, significantly reducing your tax bill for the year.

On top of that, once the well begins producing oil, the income you earn from the oil isn't taxed as conventional income. Thanks to something called depletion allowances, a portion of the oil you extract is considered to be used up over time, and you get to write off a percentage of that income as a depletion expense. This keeps your tax burden low while your investment continues to generate cash flow.

Compare that to investing in energy companies through the stock market. When you buy equities, you don't get the same tax benefits as you would by directly investing in a drilling operation. Sure, you might see your stock price increase over time, but you're still paying taxes on dividends and capital gains, and you don't get to benefit from things like IDCs or depletion allowances. That's why insider investors prefer to go directly to the source—drilling for oil—because the tax advantages can make an enormous difference in building long-term wealth.

Big Business and Brand Building: The Corporate Tax Game

Let's talk about large business for a moment. When people think of capitalism, they often think of enormous corporations like Amazon, Apple, and Google. What many people don't understand is that these companies are professionals at using the tax code to their advantage. They understand how to structure their businesses and brands to minimize taxes while maximizing profits, and they do this by aligning their goals with government incentives.

For example, large corporations are often incentivized to create employment, invest in research and development (R&D), and expand into new markets. The government rewards these activities with tax credits and deductions. When a company invests in R&D, they're authorized to deduct those expenses from their taxable income. This is why companies like Tesla and Amazon can invest billions in new technologies without paying as much in taxes as you'd expect.

Another method large corporations reduce their tax burden is through international tax strategies. Many large companies establish subsidiaries in countries with lower tax rates, allowing them to funnel profits through those subsidiaries and reduce their overall tax bill. While this strategy is often criticized, it's completely legal and is another way that corporations use the tax code to keep more of their money.

The brand building also plays a role here. When companies invest in developing a strong brand, they create an asset that generates revenue without being explicitly tied to the production of goods or services. Think about Apple. People pay a premium for Apple products, not just because of the technology, but because of the brand. Apple has built an intangible asset—its brand—that commands loyalty and higher prices. The tax code allows companies to depreciate intangible assets like patents, trademarks, and goodwill over time, further reducing their taxable income.

For small business owners, this is a vital instruction. Building a brand isn't just about increasing sales—it's about creating an asset that can increase in value and be leveraged for tax benefits. As your brand becomes more valuable, you can reinvest those profits back into your business, take advantage of tax deductions, and continue to grow without giving away a large portion of your profits in taxes.

Capitalism Rewards Action

What links all of these case studies together is the straightforward fact that the tax code rewards people who take action—whether it's investing in real estate, prospecting for oil, or developing a business. The government needs housing, energy, and employment to keep the economy running, and they rely on private individuals and companies to provide those items. In return, they offer tax incentives to those who stand up and contribute.

The key conclusion here is that the tax code isn't intended to punish you. It's a guidebook for how to build prosperity and contribute to the economy in ways that benefit both you and the country. Real estate investors benefit from depreciation. Oil and gas investors benefit from intangible extraction costs and depletion allowances. Big enterprises benefit from R&D tax credits and international tax strategies.

If you want to flourish as a capitalist investor, you need to realize that the tax code is your partner, not your enemy. It's designed to recompense those who create value—whether that's through providing housing, energy, employment, or innovation. Once you know how to use the tax code to your advantage, you'll find that capitalism is not only about making money—it's about keeping it.

Chapter 9: The Global Perspective on Taxes and Entrepreneurship

When I travel the globe and speak to audiences about taxes and entrepreneurship, I often hear the same comment: "That might work in America, but you can't do that here." Whether I'm in Russia, South Africa, Canada, Ghana, or Europe, the sentiment is the same. People believe that the opportunities available in the U.S. don't exist in their own country and that the wealthy are playing a completely distinct game. But the truth is, the principles of capitalism and tax avoidance aren't exclusive to the United States. They apply globally. It doesn't matter where you live—the rules of capitalism can work for you if you comprehend how to implement them. The tax code in every country is designed to recompense those who contribute to the economy, and those who know how to navigate it are always at an advantage.

Tax Systems Around the World: The Common Ground

Let's talk about taxes for a minute. One thing I want to make obvious is that taxes are everywhere. No matter what country you're in, the government is going to collect its share. But what most people don't realize is that tax systems all over the world are designed to reward certain behaviors—just like they are in the United States.

Governments across the globe want the same things: job creation, infrastructure development, housing, energy, and investment. And because governments can't do it all on their own, they incentivize private individuals and enterprises to take on these duties. This is where the alchemy of capitalism comes in. Whether you're in Russia, South Africa, or anywhere else, the government provides tax rebates and incentives for those who invest in the economy, create jobs, and provide essential services.

Take real estate, for example. In most countries, real estate investment comes with significant tax benefits. In the U.S., we talk about depreciation, but even in countries like Australia or the U.K., real estate investors can deduct costs like mortgage interest, maintenance, and even depreciation. In many countries, there are also incentives for those who invest in renewable energy or affordable housing, because the government requires individuals to fill those roles. The principles of using the tax code to legally avoid paying more than you need to are the same across borders.

Oil and gas investments, another sector where tax advantages are bountiful, offer similar opportunities in countries with wealthy natural resources. Whether you're drilling in Canada, Nigeria, or Saudi Arabia, tax regulations often allow for deductions related to exploration, production costs, and depletion of natural resources. The governments of these countries want to incentivize oil production, and they're willing to give tax benefits to investors who help them achieve those objectives.

Debunking the Myth: "You Can't Do That Here"

Now let's confront the myth that you can't employ these strategies outside of the U.S. I've spoken to individuals in all regions of the world, and the number one reason they believe they can't use these principles is because they've bought into the notion that their country is somehow distinct. But this simply isn't true. The norms of entrepreneurship—using money to make more money, leveraging debt, and minimizing taxes—work everywhere.

Let me share a story from my time in Russia. I was speaking at a conference, and after my presentation, a young entrepreneur came up to me and said, "**Kendra**, that's great advice for Americans, but you can't do that here in Russia. Our tax system is distinct, and the government controls everything." I smiled and told him to sit down for a moment. I asked him what his business was, and he said he owned several minor enterprises, including one in real estate. I then asked him if he took advantage of the tax deductions available for property improvements and depreciation. He appeared confused. "What deductions?" he inquired.

It turned out that Russia's tax system allows for many of the same deductions that the U.S. does, but no one had ever told him about them. He was missing out on opportunities to reduce his taxes solely because he didn't know the norms of the game. The tax code in Russia rewards those who invest in infrastructure and real estate, just like the U.S. tax code. The principles are the same—the details may differ, but the opportunities are there.

Similarly, in South Africa, I had a business proprietor tell me, "We don't have the same advantages as American companies. Our tax rates are too exorbitant, and the government takes everything." But when we looked at his business, we discovered that he wasn't taking advantage of the incentives available for creating employment and investing in local communities. South Africa offers tax incentives for businesses that employ workers, particularly in underdeveloped areas, and there are additional deductions for training and education programs. Again, the principles of entrepreneurship applied—he just didn't know how to use the system to his benefit.

In almost every country, you'll discover similar patterns. The governments want private citizens and businesses to help them accomplish national objectives, whether it's through job creation, housing, energy, or infrastructure. And because they want these things, they offer tax benefits to those who invest in these areas. The norms of capitalism operate globally.

Capitalism as a Global Force for Wealth Creation

Capitalism isn't a system that only functions in certain countries. It's a global force, and it's governed by the same principles everywhere: those who contribute to the economy by creating employment, providing housing, investing in energy, and constructing infrastructure are rewarded. And the tax system is designed to provide those rewards.

In Europe, for example, many countries offer tax incentives for renewable energy investments. If you invest in solar or wind energy, you'll often find yourself with significant tax benefits. In France, there are incentives for enterprises that invest in research and development, much like the R&D tax credits in the United States. In countries like Germany, real estate investors can deduct interest on loans, renovation costs, and depreciation, which reduces their tax liability.

Even in countries with high tax rates, like Norway or Sweden, there are opportunities to use the tax code to your advantage. In Norway, for instance, enterprises that invest in innovation or technology can obtain tax deductions. These governments may have higher taxes overall, but they still incentivize activities that contribute to economic development, and astute investors and business owners know how to take advantage of these incentives.

In every country I've visited, I've found that the principles of capitalism and tax avoidance apply. The wealthy know these principles, no matter where they live. They know how to use the tax code to create wealth, and they understand that governments will compensate them for assisting achieve national objectives. The fundamental difference between the rich and everyone else isn't the country they live in—it's the education they have about money and taxes.

Applying Global Principles to Your Situation

The lesson here is simple: it doesn't matter where you reside, the principles of capitalism and tax avoidance apply globally. The rules of the game might be slightly different, but the ultimate objective is the same: governments around the world want private individuals and businesses to help them grow their economies, and they will reward you with tax incentives for doing so.

So, if you believe you can't employ these strategies in your own country, think again. Take the time to understand the laws of your country's tax system. Talk to accountants and financial advisors who understand how to maximize tax benefits in your region. And most importantly, quit thinking like an employee and start thinking like a capitalist. The opportunities to build riches are everywhere—you just need to know how to locate them and take advantage of them.

The truth is, capitalism is a global system. It's not confined by borders or limited to specific countries. Whether you're in the U.S., Russia, UK, Ghana, China,

South Africa, or anywhere else, the principles of capitalism remain the same: those who grasp how to use money to create more money, leverage debt judiciously, and minimize taxes will succeed. The difference between those who acquire wealth and those who don't is not about where they live—it's about how they play the game.

For those who say, "You can't do that here," the reality is often that they don't completely comprehend their tax system or the opportunities that are available to them. Capitalism rewards those who take action, invest in their local economy, and contribute to the things the government values—whether it's job creation, infrastructure, or innovation. The key is to educate yourself on how your specific country's tax code works, so you can take advantage of the same opportunities that rich individuals around the globe are already using to grow their wealth.

In my experience, the true barrier isn't geography, it's mindset. Too many people limit themselves by believing that the opportunities I speak about are only available in the U.S. or only for the super-rich. But this isn't true. The principles of capitalism are available to anyone willing to learn, willing to act, and willing to see the world through the eyes of an investor, not just a laborer.

By knowing how to align your investments with government incentives—whether in real estate, energy, or business—you can significantly reduce your tax burden and build enduring wealth. The key is to stop thinking in terms of limits and start seeing the global opportunities that capitalism provides, no matter where you are.

The game is the same. The rules might alter marginally depending on the country, but the opportunities are there. You just need to be willing to understand the rules and play the game the correct way.

Chapter 10: The Future of Capitalism and Tax Strategies

The future of capitalism is always growing, and one thing you can depend on is that the tax strategies that worked yesterday might not work tomorrow. As technology continues to advance, government priorities shift, and the global economy grows more interconnected, it's critical to understand how these changes will affect your ability to build and preserve wealth.

If you're sincere about financial success, you need to stay abreast of these changes. Taxes are not static; they're dynamic, and the rich realize that to keep more of what they earn, they need to be flexible and informed. The tax code is constantly adapting to reflect new governmental priorities, emergent technologies, and societal shifts, and if you aren't paying attention, you could easily fall behind. But the good news is, that by remaining informed and proactive, you can take advantage of new opportunities as they arise.

Emerging Tax Strategies: The Role of Technology, Renewable Energy, and Government Priorities

The world is changing swiftly, and so is how you can legally minimize taxes while maximizing wealth creation. Let's talk about some of the main areas where tax strategies are emerging—technology, renewable energy, and government incentives.

First, let's look at technology. The digital age has created an entirely new world of opportunities for investors and entrepreneurs. Whether you're involved in artificial intelligence, blockchain, e-commerce, or software development, the government often offers tax incentives to companies that are stretching the boundaries of innovation. Why? Because technological advancement propels economic development. When a country fosters innovation, it strengthens its position in the global marketplace, creates employment, and enhances the overall quality of life for its citizens. That's why governments often provide tax benefits for research and development (R&D). For example, in the U.S., companies investing in R&D can qualify for considerable tax credits, reducing their tax burden by as much as 20% of their qualifying expenditures.

But here's the essential takeaway: the government rewards innovation because it promotes economic growth. If you are investing in or building enterprises in cutting-edge industries, you're not just growing your wealth—you're contributing to something much larger. And the tax code rewards you for it.

Then there's renewable energy, which is becoming more essential as governments worldwide focus on sustainability and reducing carbon footprints. The global transition towards renewable energy sources—solar, wind, and electric vehicles—has created new tax incentives. Governments want to move away from fossil fuels and are offering significant tax credits and deductions to companies and individuals investing in these technologies. For example, the Investment Tax Credit (ITC) in the U.S. allows you to deduct up to 26% of the cost of installing solar energy systems. And that's just one example. There are equivalent tax incentives for electric vehicles, energy-efficient buildings, and other renewable technologies.

The future of capitalism is bound closely to the destiny of the planet. Governments are willing to reduce your tax bill if you're willing to invest in the future. The message is clear: if you help construct a more sustainable economy, you'll be compensated financially.

Lastly, there are government priorities. Understanding where the government wants to direct its resources can give you valuable insights into future tax strategies. Right now, many administrations are focused on housing affordability, infrastructure development, and healthcare. If you're involved in these areas—whether through real estate investment, construction, or healthcare technology—you can take advantage of the tax exemptions and incentives designed to encourage growth in these sectors.

For instance, real estate developers who build affordable housing often qualify for tax credits or property tax reductions. In healthcare, there are incentives for companies that develop technologies or treatments that lower costs or improve access to care. The lesson here is simple: if you can align your investments with government priorities, the tax benefits will follow.

How to Stay Ahead: Working with Tax Professionals to Adapt to Changing Laws

Now, let's focus on how to stay ahead of the game. One of the biggest mistakes people make is presuming that they can manage their taxes on their own or relying on outdated strategies year after year. But here's the truth: the wealthy don't operate that way. They know that tax laws change, and they know that they need experts on their side to help them navigate those changes.

Working with a tax professional is not an expense—it's an investment. A competent tax advisor does more than just prepare your tax returns; they help you plan your financial future. They keep up with changing laws and trends, ensuring that you're taking advantage of every opportunity available to you.

Consider this: tax codes are thousands of pages long, and governments make amendments to those codes regularly. If you're not keeping up with those changes, you could be leaving money on the table. And as governments alter their focus—whether it's toward renewable energy, technology, or healthcare—new incentives and credits are introduced. If you don't have a professional who is tuned into these adjustments, you'll miss out.

For example, let's assume you're investing in a technology venture, and the government introduces a new tax credit for R&D expenses in that sector. If your tax advisor isn't up to date on this new credit, you could lose the opportunity to save tens of thousands, even millions of dollars, depending on the scope of your investment. This is why having a tax professional who is proactive, rather than reactive, is so critical.

Tax professionals also help you navigate international tax laws, which is becoming increasingly important as the world becomes more globalized. If you're investing in real estate or enterprises overseas, you need to comprehend how the tax codes in other countries interact with your native country's tax laws. A tax advisor with international expertise can help you structure your investments in a way that minimizes your global tax liability.

And don't assume this is just for large corporations. Whether you're a small business owner, an entrepreneur, or an investor, having the proper tax professional can make a significant difference in your ability to build and retain your wealth. The tax code is built to reward those who know how to play the game, but the rules are constantly shifting. A tax advisor helps you stay ahead of those changes and ensures that you're always operating within the law while minimizing your tax burden.

The Importance of Continual Adaptation

One thing that remains true in both life and business is that nothing stays the same eternally. The strategies that worked 10 years ago might not work today, and the strategies that work today might not work 10 years from now. The same is true with taxes. That's why it's so important to remain flexible and willing to adapt.

Many people make the error of assuming that once they have a tax strategy in place, they're set for life. But in actuality, the tax landscape is always altering. Governments change, priorities change, and new laws are passed. If you want to remain ahead, you have to be willing to modify your approach.

For example, if you've been investing in fossil fuels for years, you might discover that new regulations and tax laws make it less profitable in the future. At the same time, renewable energy investments may become more attractive as governments offer more incentives to encourage the transition to sustainable energy. In this case, it would be wise to start transferring some of your investments into renewable energy to take advantage of those new tax benefits.

The same pertains to technology. As artificial intelligence, blockchain, and other emergent technologies continue to reshape industries, governments will offer new incentives to encourage innovation. If you're not paying attention to these trends, you'll miss out on the tax benefits they offer.

That's why continual adaptation is essential. It's not just about having a tax strategy—it's about having a strategy that evolves with the times. And that's where a competent tax advisor comes in. They help you see the broader picture and alter your strategy as new opportunities arise.

The future of capitalism belongs to those who are willing to learn, adapt, and act. If you understand how taxes work and align your financial decisions with government priorities, you'll be well-positioned to build and preserve wealth in the years to come.

Conclusion: Embracing Capitalism for Financial Freedom

As we come to the close of this journey, let's take a moment to reflect on the fundamental principles of capitalism that we've explored: the power of debt, the role of taxes, and how to leverage the system to construct true financial freedom. These are the instruments of prosperity creation, and they are available to anyone willing to learn how to use them. But the truth is, most people don't. Most people spend their lives laboring for money instead of making money work for them, paying far more in taxes than they need to, and dreading debt rather than embracing it as a tool for wealth.

Debt as a Tool for Building Wealth

One of the greatest insights we've discussed is the concept of good debt. Most people have been taught to dread debt, to see it as something to avoid at all costs. However, the rich realize that not all debt is bad. Debt can be one of the most powerful tools for developing wealth—if used appropriately. Good debt is debt that places money in your purse. It's the debt you use to acquire assets that generate income, like real estate or enterprises. By leveraging excellent debt, you can control assets far more valuable than what you could afford to purchase outright, allowing you to build wealth faster.

The key is understanding the difference between good debt and poor debt. Bad debt is the kind that drains your wealth—credit card expenses, personal loans for consumption products, or anything that doesn't produce income. Good debt, on the other hand, is the kind that generates cash flow or appreciates over time. Learning to leverage good debt is one of the cornerstones of becoming a genuine capitalist.

Taxes: Your Greatest Expense—and Opportunity

We've also spent a lot of time talking about taxes. For most individuals, taxes are their primary expense, but they don't realize it. They simply assume that a substantial portion of their income goes to the government, without challenging whether there's a way to lawfully reduce that burden. But here's the truth: The wealthy don't pay as much in taxes because they know the tax code. They recognize that the tax system is designed to reward certain behaviors—behaviors that contribute to the economy and align with government priorities. And they use those rewards to keep more of what they earn.

Whether it's through investing in real estate and benefiting from depreciation, investing in oil and gas to take advantage of intangible extraction costs, or starting businesses that create employment and earn tax benefits, the wealthy know how to minimize their tax burden. They don't exploit the system—they use the system the way it was designed to be used. And that's the lesson here: Taxes don't have to be a burden. With the proper knowledge and strategy, they can become a tool for developing wealth.

Leveraging the System for Financial Freedom

At its foundation, capitalism is about leverage—using the resources and opportunities around you to create wealth. This doesn't just mean leveraging debt or taxes. It means leveraging time, knowledge, and relationships to develop a network of assets that function for you. The wealthy know that money is just one element of the equation. True wealth comes from having multiple streams of income, diversified investments, and a firm comprehension of how to use the tools of capitalism to your advantage.

The system is not fixed against you—it's available to everyone willing to learn how it functions. The problem is, that most individuals don't take the time to educate themselves. They get stuck in the mentality of working for a paycheck, trading time for money, and yearning for a comfortable retirement. But that's not what capitalism is about. Capitalism is about financial independence. It's about creating wealth that continues to grow even when you're not actively laboring for it.

The Importance of Financial Education

If there's one thing, I want you to walk away with, it's this: Financial education is the key to genuine affluence. It's not enough to labor diligently. You have to work wisely. You have to know how money works, how taxes work, how debt works, and how the system rewards those who know how to play the game. The unfortunate reality is that most people don't get this education. They go through life without understanding the fundamentals of financial literacy, and as a result, they end up working harder for less.

But it doesn't have to be that way. The knowledge is out there, and it's available to anyone who pursues it. The rich didn't become wealthy by coincidence. They became wealthy because they decided to learn how to use the instruments of capitalism—how to leverage debt, minimize taxes, and build assets. And you can do the same. It all begins with a commitment to educate yourself and take control of your financial future.

Becoming a Capitalist and Legally Reducing Your Tax Burden

So, what's the next step? It's simple: Start thinking like a capitalist. That means searching for opportunities to use debt as a tool for building wealth, finding methods to legally reduce your tax burden, and leveraging the system to create financial freedom for yourself and your family.

It means altering your perspective from being an employee—someone who works for money—to being an investor or business owner, someone who makes money work for them.

The tax code is not your enemy—it's your ally if you know how to use it. The government wants you to invest in the economy, create employment, and contribute to growth. And when you do those things, they reward you with tax incentives. Whether you're investing in real estate, energy, or enterprises, the tax code is replete with opportunities to keep more of what you earn. You just have to know where to search.

The wealthy understand this. They don't rely on a stipend. They rely on the assets they've built over time—assets that generate income, appreciate, and offer tax advantages. And the good news is, anyone can become a capitalist. It's not about being born into affluence or having a high-paying job. It's about knowing how the system functions and using it to your advantage.

The future is in your control. Take control of your financial education. Start learning about how to leverage debt, reduce your taxes, and build wealth through wise investments. Becoming a capitalist is not just for the elite—it's for anyone who is prepared to understand the rules of the game and play to win.